BODY ON THE LINE

A Collection of Poetry and Personal Essays

by Chanel Hardy

I0169267

Acknowledgements

Thank you to everyone who buys, borrows, and reads my books. I appreciate yall more than you know.

Thank you to Jennifer and Tiffany for being supportive writer friends, COFFEE WINE & WORDS wouldn't be the same without yall!

And thank you to my husband Matt, for supporting my pro-black, feminist political shenanigans all these years.

A word from the author:

If you follow me on socials or have read other non-fictional pieces by me, then you know I talk my shit. But also know that I don't talk out of my ass. Everything I write about comes from my research, whether that be in person or from doing the reading. And whenever my posts, essays, or whatever are based on anecdotal evidence, they are ALWAYS from genuine sources. I know my "hot takes" or whatever you choose to call them, may cause some animosity or negative feelings from readers. As I've said in the past, I have no control over how my words are perceived. But I want to make a few things clear:

1) You can disagree, but don't insult my intelligence as a Black woman, EVER. I deal with it enough from people in and outside the literary world who feel that you aren't allowed to be smarter than them because you don't look like them. So know your place when indulging in my space—this my shit.

2) I said what I said.

After reading this book, I hope you take what you've read and apply it somewhere that benefits marginalized women of color. Otherwise, why are you here?

Thank you for choosing this book. If you aren't familiar with me, then now is the time to get familiar.

-Chanel Hardy

Kitchen Table Talk: A Black Woman's 10 is a White Woman's 5

Growing up, it was always an ongoing joke in the black community that a black man would drop kick a Nia Long to get to a Rosie O'Donnell. The kitchen table talk about our struggles as black women being held to unfair and unrealistic beauty standards didn't immediately resonate with me as a child. I knew I was different, and I felt it. But as I reached my pre-teenage years, I was able to fully grasp the anti-blackness and how the boys at the mall would break their necks for anything with silky hair, light skin, and light eyes. I soon learned that as black girls/women we don't have the luxury of being the bare minimum.

When you're white, white adjacent, light enough to have your bloodline interrogated at the cookout, you're always a step above a black/brown-skinned/dark-skinned woman in terms of western beauty standards. A black woman's 10 is a white woman's 5. Especially if you're skinny. Especially if you're blonde. Black women don't have the luxury of a messy bun. We aren't given grace when it comes to *"I woke up like this."* For many men of color, white women are seen as a status symbol. These men feel like they've hit the genetic lottery. There is a 50/50 chance that their daughters won't face the same anti-black beauty discrimination they put us through. Instead of uplifting the skin they come from, they'd rather create something that won't have to acknowledge it at all.

And men of color aren't the only culprits of anti-blackness. White men hold the same discriminatory views on beauty when comparing their women to us. If I had a dollar for every time I heard *"You're pretty for a black girl"* or a dollar for every time I didn't hear it because I wasn't light enough with hair that looked the same going into the pool as it did coming out. No matter how hard we try, we'll never be enough in a society that says *white is right*. A culture that says light skin is the only shade deserving of love and respect.

I recall a gathering at my cousin's house as a child. My mom and I were in the living room with our two cousins watching TV, and a news story came on about Wesley Snipes owing the government taxes. My cousin Bernadette said something along the lines of *"Oh well, I don't feel bad for him. He don't like us anyway. You know they only like those white women."* I remember at that moment wondering what about being black made us undesirable? As we often see with wealthy black male entertainers and athletes, white partners become the main course in their dating pool. This goes back to the status symbol of having white partners.

Even if a white woman has a plethora of children, no job, and no pot to piss in, she'll be chosen over a black woman with a six-figure career who abides by all the morals we are conditioned to follow. The rules of what is socially acceptable are different for us. The idea is that the status symbol of dating white women somehow erases or eases the burden of racism. But in reality, it does the opposite. It upholds the oppressive structures and becomes a breeding ground for fetishization and colorism. So, in the end, black women are still stuck at the bottom. Then who will be left to uplift us? We have to uplift each other. At the kitchen table. Have a seat, sis.

Blue Eyes

Blue eyes are the reason why the comb pulls at my scalp

why my momma tells me to stop crying before she gives me something to cry about

blue eyes are the reason why the popular girl pulled my scarf off in gym class in the seventh grade and laughed

everyone laughed

blue eyes are the reason why I cut the hair off my black barbie doll to make them Kens when my white barbies didn't get a boyfriend for Christmas

blue eyes are the reason why I never got a boyfriend for Christmas

blue eyes are the reason why I wrote Emily's name in the back of my borrowed library book in first grade instead of my own name because I wanted to be her

Emily didn't have blue eyes, but someone along the lines of her biracial gene pool did

those blue eyes, the ones our ancestors stared into all those centuries ago when the Europeans first cracked the whip and told them that his blue eyes would haunt their children and grandchildren and set the rules for their daughters and granddaughters self-esteem

blue eyes are the reason why I wrote this poem

why I write at all

why it's important for Black women and girls to know that even without blue eyes, we are the blueprint

the beauty that reigns supreme.

.

Body on the Line

You ask us to fight for you
Put our bodies on the line for good morning texts and
"McDonald's is a date"

You ask us to go against the police state
our values, our independence

All so you can say that we never had your back
We don't love you
Never did

We just want what's in your pockets
Loose change in the cigarette

We're starting to feel like you don't really want
change
You want power

Power over our bodies
The same bodies you lay against and beg for
forgiveness

And we give it
Every single time
Every single lie

Every single woman who ever said she was fine being
a single woman

Because the truth is as women we don't benefit from
marriage like men do

We were born to nurture
Trained for servitude straight from the womb

The truth is we've always put our bodies on the line
for you

But what have you done for us?

Watching Jennifer's Body and the Blood Still Won't Come Off

You know that scene when emo Adam Brody stabs an innocent teenage girl and throws the murder weapon down that hole?

I wondered how many more women were sacrificed and tossed away in Devil's Kettle

Their bodies rotting in an endless stream of water
The cops would've never found Jennifer's body rotting in that endless stream of water

What does it say about the world girls live in when a demon gives you more autonomy than a human being?

What does it mean when the only time her body could function was when she had the flesh of a man to keep her from crumbling?

Even in death, she needed a boy to keep her from dying.
What kind of life is that?

Hell is a teenage girl and Devil's Kettle is where their souls go to die.

In the end, Jennifer got justice, if that's what you want to call it.

But in real life, girls whose bodies rot in an endless stream of water don't get justice.

When the credits roll, the movie is over but the blood still won't come off.

{seen on Facebook. 6.11.22}

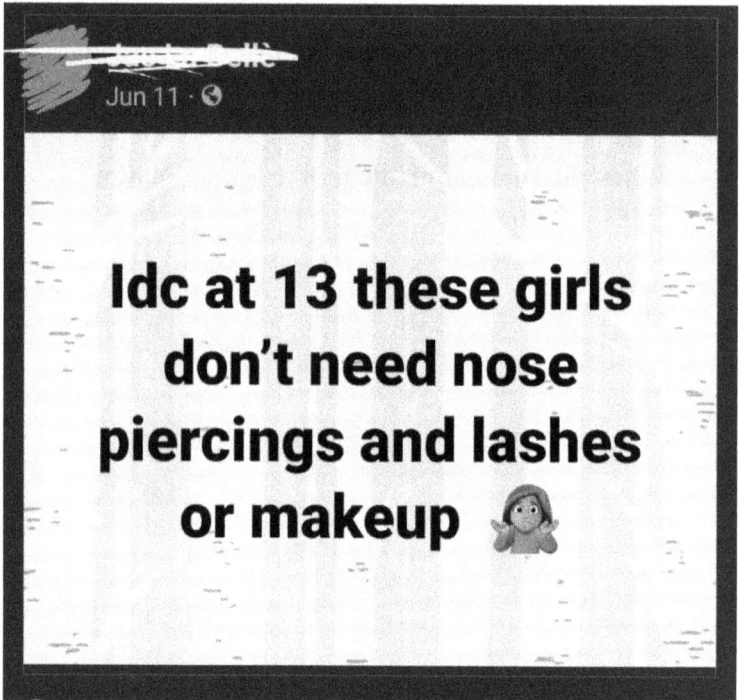

…or a mouth
or eyes
or skin
or arms
or legs
or a liver
or a uterus

or a heart
because misogyny says teenage girls don't deserve
anything.

The Girl Who Lives There

You don't have to tell a woman she's gained weight
every time you see her

She knows because she lives there
In her own body

She can hear her thighs touch when she walks
The sound her heart makes at the beginning of every
doctor visit

The laughs from men whose entire personality is
never dating fat women
And the cat calls from men who only like her when
their heads are between her legs

She didn't invite you into her home so you could
point out the flaws inside of it

You don't think she knows?
She lives there

In the house that God built

She wakes up every morning and does her daily
rituals making sure the cracks are properly mended

Making sure that nothing leaks
Making sure the foundation is strong enough to last
another 60 years

Her body is her forever home

No need to speak on what goes on within walls and
which you do not live

She knows.

Tell Me Where It Hurts

The doctor asks where I hurt
I say everywhere but mainly in my lower legs

The doctor asks if I'm drinking enough water
The doctor asks if I walk enough
The doctor asks if I get enough exercise
If I'm eating well and taking my vitamins

I say yes
I say yes
I say yes

The doctor doesn't ask about my mental health
The doctor just asks me to get on the scale

The numbers go up and my doctor asks if I want these
pamphlets on nutritional help

When I didn't get my period for 7 months the doctor
didn't ask about my mental health
If I had been depressed or stressed

But on the inside I say yes
I say yes
I say yes

When I was suffering with UTI symptoms the doctor
didn't ask if I was peeing 20 times a day
Or if my lower abdominal pain kept me up at night

But the doctor did ask me about my blood pressure

And I just said I was nervous because you know
going into the doctor's office when you're a fat bitch
is never fun

Neither is having high blood pressure

Speaking of high blood pressure
I had a breast cancer scare in 2020

And when I went to the doctor they asked about my
blood pressure twice

The doctor took my blood pressure twice
The doctor said *"you're too young to have breast
cancer but about that blood pressure..."*

Every time I go to the doctor now I already know
what to expect
So I put my crossbody bag on the nurses table before
I step on the scale

And I say yes
I say yes
I say yes.

Upload, heart-react
Won't tell her she's beautiful
So her heart reacts

Curly, silk-press, bob
Leave in for 20 minutes
Remove, rinse, repeat.

Kitchen Table Talk: Amy Schumer Bitches

What is it with white women who make hating their plus-size bodies their entire personality? And I don't mean unpacking fatphobia in a valid way, but like, the Amy Schumer bitches. Y'all know what I mean. I talk about the crappy experiences of being fat but not in a way that's generally derogatory towards fat women. What I mean is that it's okay to lament our troubles having bigger than the beauty standard bodies. But at what point do our complaints become harmful, at the expense of other women? Let me make one thing clear; I hate being fat "sometimes." I hate not being able to find cute clothes over an XL or paying significantly more on rare occasions when I do. I hate being unable to accommodate my gut in bright colors and tight outfits. I hate when a top fits perfectly, but the arms are too tight. But I don't hate my body. Despite all the things it puts me through.

Being a size 16/18, my feelings toward my body have pretty much been the same since I was a size 10/12. A decade ago. And I know what you're probably thinking. *"A size 12?? That's not even fat!"* While I agree that size and weight are debatable, the US sizing standards consider anything over a 12 to be plus-size. This means that you have generations of women who grew up believing that being a size 12 meant they were one cheeseburger away from being on My 600 lb Life.

Interestingly, this mentality has been more prevalent among non-Black and non-Latino women. For example, in a black household, being a size 12 is considered curvy. But white women aren't given that same grace in their communities. So you end up with Amy Schumer bitches.

If you're familiar with Amy Schumer, then you know she's a white female comedian who got her big break on Comedy Central in 2013 with her television sketch show, 'Inside Amy Schumer.' I remember watching a couple of episodes back then, And I thought it was pretty funny. Some of the material was relatable. Not necessarily the parts about being fat but just the quirkiness of being a woman in general. But that didn't last long.

Her entire appeal has thrived on the idea that while white women hate being fat, they sure love to profit off it. I recall Amy getting frustrated with media outlets referring to her as plus size when she didn't consider herself a "fat woman." Meanwhile, she had no issues making fun of her experiences being considered fat in what I assume was a half-assed attempt at tackling fatphobia.

Instead of her concerns coming from a genuine place, it felt like she had difficulty coming to terms with herself. Like many white women who deal with fatphobia, Amy's take on body shaming was more like *"I'm not one of those fat bitches"* instead of *"Maybe as a society, we need to rethink how we criticize and categorize women's bodies."* I'm sure her heart was in the right place, but her approach never sat right with me.

And it's not just Amy. White women collectively contribute to fatphobia more than they rally against its harmful stigmas. And in most cases, I'm sure this is not intentional. One of the ways I observe this phenomenon is on social media. Recently I was scrolling through my Instagram timeline when I came across a post that read something along the lines of *"Instead of hot girl summer, we're having a chubby girl summer..." *GAG**

I must let it be known that I think these types of posts are corny as hell. First, it insinuates that chubby girls are not also hot. Which we know is false. Secondly, It attempts to hijack and completely misses the point of the Hot Girl Summer movement, coined by rapper Meg Thee Stallion. Do you see what I mean? Their attempts at being quirky and making "fat" acceptable are just lame and pointless.

White women have also become the face of the body positivity movement, leaving women of color in the dark to fend for ourselves. What makes this so frustrating is that they have only embraced being plus-sized for maybe the past 20 years. Meanwhile, for generations, black women have been screaming from the rooftops about how we love our plus-size bodies. So how come a community of women got the authority to speak for all of us when they pick and choose when to be on our side? I don't know about you, But I think it's about damn time Black women snatch the mic back from the Amy Schumer bitches of society and give the body positivity movement the real TLC it needs.

That White Feminist in Blue Jeans

Fuck her
and the centrists who post *'All lives matter'*
and fill their feeds with coded bigotry

stealing quotes from 2012 Tumblr
who say *"hey I'm not white! My great-grandfather's
rape victim was Navajo!"*
while they benefit from white privilege and support
us colored folk when it's convenient

black bodies on the gram
exploiting our trauma for self-gain
they like black dick so that's enough proximity to
keep them relevant

enough distance to keep them detached

white allyship is
often performative
often
always
useless.

Fucked

There is no consent under fascism.
no body autonomy in a place that owns you.
you lie back and take it
while he strokes the freedom from your hair
holds you down by the wrists
and whispers *"How do you like this white dick?"*
when it's over, you clean yourself up
he counts his money
Self-righteous and placid
he gets what he wants
and you don't get shit
ain't got shit
won't ever have shit
not under this nation
ran by the good ol' boys and the capitalists
a revolution is coming, I feel it
won't be long now
your time will come
no more being fucked by fascism
we will rise, we will end it
together.

Fetishization is...

Fetishization is when you let your high school
boyfriends best friend feel you up at a party

It's when you can't meet the family but you can hang
out in the middle of the night

Fetishization is when they love the idea of you but an
idea doesn't equal respect
They thrive on a fantasy of what it would taste like to
violate you

A body can be violated and more than just the
physical way

A body becomes violated when you stop going
outside in the summer because he likes you dark...
but not too dark

A body becomes violated when you're afraid of losing
weight because you've attached yourself worth to
#TeamBBW groups on Facebook

The minute you second guess any decision in your
life for the sake of a romantic partner's approval
you've been violated

Fetishization has a funny way of showing its true
colors

Even through the best intentions

And it extends past romantic pursuits
children can be fetishized too

And more often than not we see this with interracial
couples and white people who adopt black and brown
children

They obsess over features and stereotypes with a
white savior complex

Black parents want daughters whose curls stretch
across the Atlantic

With light eyes that sparkle like crisp ocean waters

They don't want the burden of having children they
can't put on a pedestal

Fetishization puts us on a pedestal we never ask to be
on

It demands us to meet expectations as a shot of
dopamine
Fetishization is dopamine

A chemical imbalance of the brain

A person sees someone they want and convinces
themselves that person is not a person
But a personal goal

Fetishization is when your high school boyfriend's best friend feels you up at a party

And you don't do anything about it.

Kitchen Table Talk: It's Not You, It's Him: Manipulation in Gender Dynamics

Men who seek sexual relationships intentionally pursue women who make it clear that they want romance and commitment. They lead us on, doing and saying all the right things to get us where they want us. But after the sex, the inevitable happens. We never hear from Mr. Perfect again. Women often blame themselves and wonder where things went wrong on their end. But the issue is never actually us. It all boils down to toxic masculinity, how men view women and taking pride in the manipulative games they play.

I used to ask myself why these men never pursue women who want what they want. Women who are comfortable with their sexuality and enjoy the perks of casual sex. That's when it dawned on me that doing so would put a dent in their fragile egos. For men, sex is almost always about control. The only time men enjoy sex with sexually liberated women is when they pay for it. This way, they maintain the illusion that they are the ones in control. As a result, a woman free from social conventions regarding her body is labeled a whore. All while men are free to live a similar lifestyle with no judgment.

But it's not just about sexism and control. Men get a sick sense of pleasure from leading women on. It's emotionally damaging, preventing women from putting their complete trust in future partners. This also causes a shift in gender dynamics as time passes. Women become more emotionally withdrawn, trying to remain one step ahead of the men they date. But I wouldn't necessarily consider this a bad thing. Beating men at the games they play has given women a new sense of power, causing the opposite sex to rethink their player strategies, and put themselves in the shoes of those they hurt. Regardless of how you choose to handle these situations, remember that we've all been there, we've all bounced back from it, and you will too.

Kitchen Table Talk: Racist Beauty Standards Didn't Begin with Us

I'm sure you've seen The Princess Diaries starring Anne Hathaway and Julie Andrews. Or maybe you've read the book by Meg Cabot. One of Mia's main issues in this story is her physical appearance. She's considered unattractive, dorky, and invisible to her peers at school. Now, being a Black girl watching this movie and reading the book, I didn't quite understand what was so unattractive about Mia Thermopolis. She had big, poofy curls and wore glasses. Big deal. But that was exactly it. Her curly hair and glasses. *(I recall there being a mention of her nose too, but I could be wrong. It's been a while.)*

After Mia got her makeover, which included bone-straight hair and contacts, her world instantly changed. She was treated better by the popular girls at school. She even got noticed by her crush. All because of a good flat iron. The Princess Diaries was one of the first times I noticed how white women deal with beauty standards that stem from white supremacy.

Yes, you heard that correctly. Women of color aren't the only ones who deal with racist beauty standards. I know you're probably wondering what that has to do with us. It has everything to do with us, because if women who are already on top of the beauty standard totem pole still deal with these issues, then what does that say about the rest of us? If a white woman is considered unattractive because she has curly hair, then what does that say about Black women who have the kinkiest of coils? Well, it says a lot, actually. There are several ways in which white women deal with beauty standards with roots tied to white supremacy.

Big noses. White folks have a history of making derogatory remarks and jokes about 'Jewish noses.' Even if you aren't Jewish, having a big nose as a white person associates you with having Jewish or middle eastern ancestry.

Curly hair. As I described in my example above with The Princess Diaries, curly hair is often seen as unruly or less attractive in white women. Similar to big noses, many believe that dark curly hair links back to Jewish or middle eastern ancestry. In other words, any smidge of a trace that you could possibly come from a person of color is deemed less attractive according to white beauty standards.

The hyper-feminization of and the preferences for blonde hair. (The blonde v.s brunette rivalry in media.) This one was always a mystery to me. White folks treat hair color like it's an ethnicity. I've heard white men say they have preferences for blondes or only date blondes and it never sits right with me. What about a hair color makes a woman more or less attractive? Are they not still white at the end of the day? This preference has also felt very coded to me. Considering the only people who are naturally born with blonde hair are white, what are you really saying? *(Yeah I know about those brown indigenous people from that photo ya'll share every month. Don't get cute, you know what I mean LOL.)*

Blue Eyes. The sign of pure white blood. Right along with blonde hair. Again, any smidge of a trace that you could possibly come from a person of color is deemed less attractive according to white beauty standards. Now brown eyes are obviously the most common of eye colors in the world. So having brown eyes isn't discriminated against as much these days, if at all.

This in no way means that as a white woman reading this, you should take this as a sign to take up space where you don't belong, or make these issues about you. The point of me sharing this was to highlight how much these beauty standards affect women of color, especially Black women. If you found any of these examples relatable, then just sit with that for a moment. Think about the issues Black women face, and how harmful and extreme they are for us.

She is…

She is chocolate
she is brown sugar
she is maple syrup
she is almond
she is cinnamon
she is mocha
she is molasses
she is hickory
She is coffee, no cream
she is cafe au lait
she is cafe noir
she is caramel
she is chestnut
she is chickpeas
she is everything but human.

Niggas Always Gotta Cat-call a Bitch

"It must be jelly cuz jam don't shake like that!"

It must be worms because I know you don't kiss your
mother with that mouth.

It must be the audacity because you done lost your
damn mind!

It must be the crack in your skull the doctor left
pulling too hard when you were born because I am
not your bitch.

It must be the toxic masculinity rotting your brain.

It must be that your momma never held you close
enough and taught you how to respect a woman.

Or it must be me.
Wearing that dress that makes my ass look good.
My curves just right.

No, it must be you.
Using your words to violate a stranger.

Kitchen Table Talk: Representation in Media

We live in the era of the Incel v.s the Blue Haired
Feminist. The social justice warriors vs. the not-so-
politically correct conservative patriots. So if you
spend enough time on social media, (or at family get-
togethers during the holidays) then you're familiar
with the issues surrounding race and sexual
orientation in the media. In the past decade, there has
been a trend of movies, and TV shows that seem to
intentionally aim at marginalized audiences. For
example, the all-female remake of the 2016
Ghostbusters movie, the all-black remake of Steel
Magnolias that aired in 2012, and the 2015 remake of
Annie, featured a multi-racial cast and a black girl
Quvenzhané Wallis, portraying little orphan Annie.

But it's not just film remakes jumping on the trend,
The Last Jedi director Rian Johnson spoke on how he
is all for more diversity in film, specifically the recent
Star Wars movies which have gotten media attention
for trying to be politically correct in their casting
choices. Even the recent shows on Disney Plus such
as 'Obi Wan' have faced backlash over its new Black
female antagonist. Some people feel that forced
diversity and inclusion, or how they like to put it,
"new age affirmative action" is silly and unnecessary.
While on the opposite end, others believe that

Hollywood is long overdue for some real diversity and inclusion in TV and film. Specifically in genres like sci-fi and fantasy where people of color, mainly Black women are known to be left out or "Token." Franchises like Harry Potter are one of many to be criticized in the past for not featuring enough people of color, or re-casting and race swapping. Star Wars can't even have a black woman as a villain or main character without the white fanboys going crazy. We cannot exist in media without it being seen as a political agenda. The worst part is women of color are rarely ever defended in these situations. We tolerate abuse and harassment from strangers with no help from our peers. If you recall, Kelly Marie Tran, an actress from the 2017 Star Wars film faced racist harassment so severe, that it drove her off social media.

But it's not just TV and film, some people of color and the LGBTQ community feel that books also tend to lack a fair representation of them. It's hard to find books that center around these people that aren't filled with stigmas and stereotypes, even when written by their own demographics. People of color are sick of being fetishized. Black boys want to be wizards too, and queer black girls want real love stories that aren't erotic and written for the pleasure of horny men.

I conducted a study on diversity and inclusion in most forms of media, where participants were of different ages, genders, and from different racial backgrounds. **11%** of respondents said that women of color are equally represented in most forms of media, while **88%** said they are not. When it comes to men of color, **33%** said that they are equally represented, while **66%** said no. When it came to who was the least represented, women of color held the top spot with **66%** of respondents saying they were, followed by men of color at **22%** and white women at **11%**. White men and women were close when asked who represented the most. **55%** of respondents said that white men were, while the other **44%** felt it was white women.

I also asked if people felt that the LGBTQ community was equally represented. **66%** said no, while **33%** said yes. Out of the **66%** that said no, more than half feel that LGBTQ women of color have the worst. It's also important to note the gender differences in these studies. While most agreed that people of color, in general, are not represented equally, **11%** of black men feel that men of color, especially those that are LGBTQ are often left out.

But regardless of people having different opinions on the representation of different groups, one thing all participants agreed on, was that even when these groups of people are portrayed, negative stereotypes are a common issue, which takes the movement of equality two steps forward but five steps back. As a woman of color myself, I can assure you that it is so important for people to be able to see themselves in a positive and unique light when watching TV and reading books. It's important to break down cultural barriers while at the same time, still allowing people to feel connected within their own. Stepping outside of racial and gender stereotypes, and redefining what it means to be black, male or female, or gay.

I Am Not My Hair by India.Arie

████, I can kinda recall ████████
Small, t█████████████████ black
A███████████████████t flat
████ lumpy ████████████
J████████
Nappy headed b███████
████████████
████████████████████crazy
(crazy)
████████████████
████████████████████
█████████████s█████████
██████████
All these girls ███████████
█████████████so flawed
████████████████
████████████████
██████████████
██████████████
A█████████████on
█████████████
█████████████
███████████████
P████ it was time to change ████
████████the woman that I am inside
████████████all gone
█████████████████████

A body hears all
can taste when it's neglected
can feel when you don't love it
a body knows when it's an afterthought
existing out of obligation.

{seen on twitter. 6.24.22}

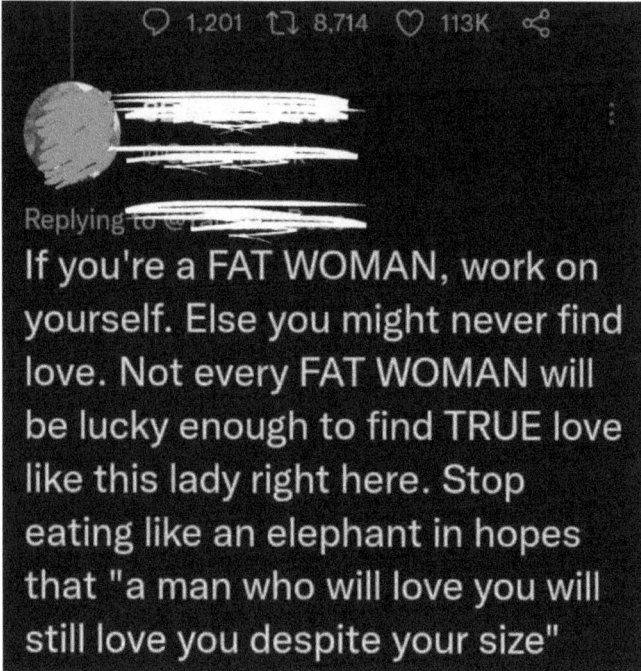

If you're a FAT WOMAN, work on yourself. Else you might never find love. Not every FAT WOMAN will be lucky enough to find TRUE love like this lady right here. Stop eating like an elephant in hopes that "a man who will love you will still love you despite your size"

If you're a fat woman, love is unattainable unless you suck in your gut and hide every flaw that a man might see

Pull the fat in your face back with razor wire so he can see you smile while you starve on a $20 date

Not every fat woman will be lucky enough to settle for scraps and a small dick like their skinny friends

But maybe if we all stopped eating like elephants then men we don't even like will like us, right?

Kitchen Table Talk: Invasion of the Booty Snatchers

Nothing reminds me of my age like pop culture. I can still recall the very first time I heard about Kim Kardashian. On my way to school, I was in the car with my mom, and Ray J's sex tape had just leaked. Everyone knew who he was at the time, but no one knew her. The one thing the radio host mentioned was how this Armenian mystery beauty had a big booty. Before I even saw a picture of Kim, I already knew that her ass was her signature feature. Now in retrospect, I don't think her ass was that big before the plastic surgery. But the standards for what was considered a fat ass were very low at the time. Especially when having an ounce of fat and/or curves was outrageous in Hollywood and the music industry. It also needs to be clarified that a nice ass and a fat ass are two completely different things.

I think it's safe to assume that Kim Kardashian led the crusade of white women embracing big booties and curvier figures. And now, nearly 15 years later, It's become a beauty trend. I won't call it a beauty "standard" because that implies all who assimilate will benefit from it—which we do not. And assimilation is not the same as appropriation. *Assimilation* is when minorities are forced to adopt features from a dominant culture in order to fit in and survive. *(Black women straightening our hair for jobs/hair discrimination in the workplace)* **Appropriation** is the unacknowledged adoption of elements of a culture or identity. Not required for survival but copied as a trend. *(Non-Black women wearing cornrows, Non-Japanese women wearing geisha styles without understanding why it's harmful.)*

The funny thing is, being over 30, I can still remember a time when being curvy was not socially acceptable for women outside of the black (and, in some cases, Latino) community. But those coming of age now have no idea.

Recently Jennifer Lopez, a celebrity well-known for having a booty in the '90s, did an interview where she spoke on what it was like being considered curvy in the industry. She shared experiences where it hurt her acting career. Her passion for acting wasn't taken seriously by casting directors, hurting her chances of getting prominent leading roles. As we know, Jennifer is known for some reasonably good movies—and others not so good. But it's interesting to think about what kind of acting career she would have had if it weren't for the fatphobia in Hollywood. When Jennifer's interview was shared, many denied her experiences simply because they found them unbelievable. I saw comments like,

"Everybody loved her ass back in the day."

"All the men loved her big booty!"

"She just wants attention."

What these people don't realize is that how you are perceived as a woman on the street and sexually by strangers is not how you are perceived when it comes to your career. Of course, Jennifer was praised for having a nice ass. But I don't doubt for one second that her experience was completely different in front of the big wigs of Hollywood trying to play a white woman in some typical run-of-the-mill Oscar-bait film. Jennifer Lopez spent most of her film career doing rom-coms. Although they suit her well, in my opinion, I don't think this is a coincidence.

But this isn't really about Jennifer. It's about how black features like a fat ass and big lips were once frowned upon by a demographic who seems to want to dominate this beauty trend now. The ones who gave women like Jennifer Lopez a hard time 20 years ago are encouraging white women to get plastic surgery and fillers to mimic what they once hated. So much so, If you tell a 16-year-old that these features used to be considered ugly, they'll think you're lying. But the unfortunate truth is that certain features are still only preferred on white or white-adjacent women over black women. *(For those who do not know what white-adjacent means, it refers to people who may not be considered ethnically/culturally white but are still white-passing. Such as non-Black Latinos, some eastern Europeans, Southeast Asians, etc..)*

It's gotten to the point where blackfishing has become a new phenomenon. **Blackfishing** is when non-black women alter their features in a way that makes them intentionally ambiguous or straight up look like a Black person. This is done with makeup techniques, cosmetic surgery, wearing ethnic hairstyles such as box braids, and even skin tanning to questionable shades. You've probably also heard of asianfishing, which is the same thing but with the features of an Asian woman. Ariana Grande was recently accused of this. Apparently, she had surgery done with the skin around her eyes to make them look stretched? I'm not Asian, so that's not my lane. But you can find posts on Twitter and TikTok from Asian women who have spoken up about this.

The recent popularity of AAVE among Gen z aged folk has added another layer to the blackfishing fiasco, also known as digital black face. When people who are not black hide behind Black avis and/or create fake social media personalities to mimic a black person. It seems that black people, mainly black women, are copied in every aspect of our existence. Nothing we do is deemed socially acceptable until the Kardashians of the world get a hold of it. Not our bodies, our language, or our culture. In the words of the late Paul Mooney, "Everybody wanna be a nigga but don't nobody wanna be a nigga."

Kitchen Table Talk: "She Got That Good Hair!"

In 2018, the *Nappily Ever After* book-to-film adaptation starring Sanaa Lathan made its debut on Netflix. Based on the 2000 book by Trisha Thomas, this movie tells the story of Venus Johnston, a young black woman with a thriving career, a handsome boyfriend, and a rich social life. However, she has an emotional breakdown over relationship troubles and shaves her head. Venus grew up like many black girls did, including me. Our hair always had to be a certain way, and we were a representation of our parents 24/7. Being "nappy" was never acceptable under any circumstances. If you got your hair wet, life was over! So, of course, like most of us, Venus took these perceptions into adulthood, where her appearance— specifically her hair, consumed her life. I must say, her post-haircut character development felt unrealistic. For a woman who spent her entire life obsessing over being the perfect woman, she adjusted to rocking the bald look WAY TOO EASILY! No wig phase? Yeah right! Halfway through the film, I felt like I was watching a completely different movie. She went from wearing a silk scarf to work out of embarrassment to giving "You're beautiful just the way you are" advice to a little girl within a week. All in all, I gave the film three out of five stars. But I still recommend it.

When I first cut my hair in 2010, I rocked a wig in public the first year, and I was nowhere near as obsessed about my appearance as Venus was in that film. Being bald and going natural for the first time came with several bouts of insecurity and second-guessing my decision. I chose to cut my hair after a bad experience getting a texturizer while still having a relaxer. My hair was a patchy mess! So two days later, at my now-husband Matthew's house, I took his beard trimmer and shaved my head. It was a glorious experience, and to this day, it was one of the best decisions I have ever made. I felt like I could do anything. If I could step outside the box and go against one of the most challenging expectations as a Black woman—to assimilate my hair, then I was unstoppable. I had gotten relaxers since I was seven years old. But now, it was just me, my hair, and a new outlook on life.

Once my natural coils began to grow, I was excited to try new products and experiment with new hairstyles. I quickly realized that the issues I was freeing myself from by going natural still existed within that community. Instead of straight v.s nappy, I had entered the world of 3a v.s 4c. The looser the curl, the cuter the girl. The hair chart *(as shown in the following pictures)* begins at 1a, bone straight, and ends at 4c, the kinkiest of coils. My hair is 4c.

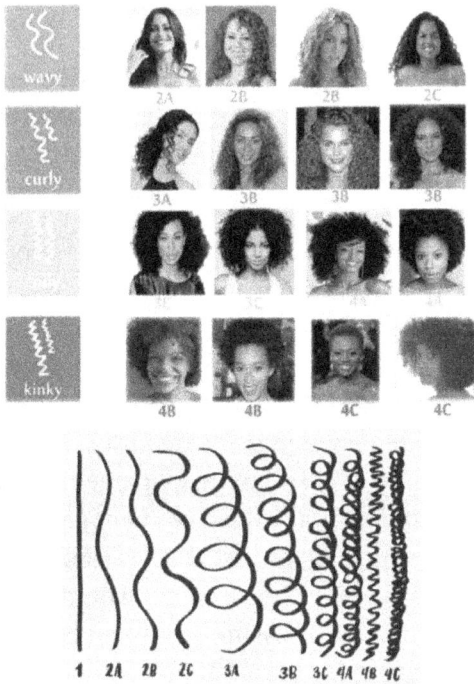

One of the first products I tried was a curling custard by Kinky Curly, a line of natural hair products. I looked up photos and YouTube videos on women using the product and felt like I could give it a shot to loosen up my curl pattern and make my hair more flexible. Now, this was my first mistake. As a natural, you first must understand that your hair is gonna do what it's gonna do. No amount of manipulation without a permanent chemical will change your hair's natural form. If it does, it's only temporary and not worth the effort. Especially when you factor in weather conditions. I'm sorry ma'am, but you ain't getting a Tracie Ellis Ross fro with 4c coils. It ain't happening! So all those creams, smoothies, and custards marketed to us are pointless. *(And I wish they would stop naming this shit after food. It's corny as hell.)*

Don't get me wrong, some of the products do what they intend, but not for every curl pattern. Most of the products you see on the shelves today are for the 3a/b/c girls. Not for us with nappier curl patterns. A movement that was meant to uplift Black women's natural hair still left out a vast majority of us by playing into the white supremacy game. Between 2011-2015, the natural hair movement gained tons of support and followers as hair relaxer sales decreased for the first time in decades. Black women were breaking the chains of assimilation and embracing our natural hair again for the first time since the civil rights movement. But this also came with tons of challenges. After decades of not knowing our hair in its natural form, many women had similar experiences as I did. We searched all over the web for products and tutorials to tame our hair. The movement became less about health and embracing our hair as it grew and became more about length and having looser curls. So much so that even now, I never grow my hair past an inch without getting a texturizer. (If you don't know what those are, they are basically curly perms. But specifically for short hair.)

I never claimed to be perfect when embracing my natural hair. Since my first big chop twelve years ago, I've grown my hair back on more than one occasion. The last time was 2018. Sometimes being natural gets boring, and I want to feel like Beyonce. Other times I love being bald and on my Amber Rose shit. But regardless of what I choose, I never forget that I am not my hair. The natural hair movement had a grip on Black women so tight that I feel like we lost ourselves in something that was meant to do the opposite. We became obsessed with trying to prove our Blackness and authenticity instead of just having fun and being the bad bitches we are. Do I recommend going natural and doing a big chop? ABSOLUTELY! Even if you don't keep it. But shackles are still shackles. Your hair is not in charge. You are. So throw out that basket of curly ketchup and mustard that you used one time eight years ago *(don't act like you ain't got one sis!)* and show yourself some love.

Bald Headed Hoe *ish

I shave my head
and I feel like I'm the baddest bitch in the room

whenever I cut my hair, all my problems hit the floor
i can think clearly

the boulders weighing me down crumble and vanish
when I shave my head, I am thirty pounds lighter
my skin is ten times smoother

my lips a little plumper
my ass a little bit bigger

fifteen years ago, a shaved head meant life was over
but now?

a shaved head means you've lived a thousand lives
and felt love a thousand times over.

An Untitled Poem about Self Love or Some Shit

One has hair of silk
The other cotton

One has the skin of pink blush
The other skin of bronze armor

He takes one by the hand and whispers love songs
He takes the other by the hand and whispers *"call me daddy."*

He plans out a life with one
While planning next Saturday night with the other

One girl gets a lifetime of promises, a home,
extravagant trips
The other gets to trip about a man who didn't even
remember her birthday

But a bad bitch never trips
She books trips and spoils herself

Wine and dine like she's the prize
You are the prize
The ultimate dream girl, so fly and flawless

You never needed no man's validation to reach the
stars

No hair like silk

Or skin like cream
But a body like no other
A vibe like no other

And that smile
Pucker those lips and stretch those teeth because the
mirror never lies

You don't need to be what a man wants you to be
To feel loved
To feel free.

Chanel Hardy

Captain Hook by Megan Thee Stallion

I'm a problem

a bitch

my style
my hair

I'm a Hot Girl,
I wear the shit

, now,
with a little bit of curve

The Hairy Pussy Chronicle

When I shaved for the first time
the razor in my right hand
shaving cream in my left
my parents left the house so it was just me
and my hairy pussy

I was 11
halfway through puberty and halfway out of my mind
because I knew absolutely nothing about how to
shave my pussy

but what I did know was that boys didn't like hairy
pussy
it was disgusting
vile
I was an animal covered in filth and human fur

At 11 I had no interest in sex per se
but I knew that when girls had sex the boys they had
sex with didn't like hairy pussies

so, I covered my crotch and skintimate scented
women's shaving gel and shaved away

I was becoming a woman
the good kind of woman
the good kind of woman that didn't have a hairy pussy

Unfortunately, nobody told this good kind of woman
how to shave her pussy properly

so I shaved the wrong way and ended up looking like
the backside of a crunch bar

Welcome to your new problem!
my new problem, *ingrown hairs galore!*

The only thing worse than a hairy pussy for a preteen
girl growing up with the patriarchy was an ugly pussy

Poor preteen girl

Growing up with the patriarchy telling her that she's
not worthy of love unless she removes the things that
make her woman
makes her human
makes ME human

Now that 11-year-old girl
is a 31-year-old woman who couldn't care less about a
hairy pussy

Or who likes hairy pussy
or who has sex with the girls or the boys who don't
like hairy pussy

The good news is
When you become an adult
nobody actually gives a fuck about hair on a pussy

The good news is
it's your choice and nobody else's

The good news is
I did eventually learn to shave properly

Negro Woman for Sale

Sometimes I think about my ancestors
my great great great grandmothers

sweating on the fields, calloused hands

their blood leaving stains on the legacies of their
masters

their blood leaving stains on the sheets they had to
clean

the sheets they were violated on
Birthed babies on

those babies wrapped in those blankets and carried off
to be sold
never seen again

breasts sore and swollen
bodies depleted after the birth of a nation

babies stolen

now mama must use her body to nurse her master's
wife's babies

my ancestors didn't even own their own bodies
not their hands, mouths, ovaries
breast milk

every single part of my ancestors bodies had a price
tag

there is no body autonomy when your body is
livestock
my ancestors

my great great great grandmothers
great grandmothers

aunts
sisters
wives
daughters

put their bodies on the line
sold their bodies long before sex work or selling your
body had a name.

I Eat My Feelings but She Doesn't Have To

PMS says anxiety/says eat this cake/says drink these calories/PMS says you spelled my name wrong/It's nice to meet you I'm PMDD/Anxiety says you can't go out today/because reasons/because you look like shit actually/actually those shorts are too small/that shirt is too tiny/you're not tiny/so why are you leaving the house in that outfit?/I guess I'll stay inside/I'll stay inside and eat my feelings/watch videos on how to eat better/videos on how to manage/my weight/my anxiety/my PMS/PMDD?/but those videos/the women in the videos hardly eat at all/but they claim they have all the answers/and I'm wondering where the answers are/underneath those size 4 jeans/underneath that crop top/behind those narrow cheekbones/the answer is she's just pandering for the algorithm/my hostess donuts don't pander to me/so maybe I'll just keep those by my side for comfort instead.

Chanel Hardy

It {Begins}Ends with Us

I've spent my entire life trying to figure out what
beauty truly means. I don't think anyone ever called
me pretty or attractive in any way until I had finished
puberty. By that time, the attraction boys felt towards
me was mostly sexual. It was all driven by hormones.
It never felt romantic or genuine. Not even
platonically. For a lot of black girls growing up, being
beautiful was something only reserved for girls with
specific features. The light-skinned or biracial girls.
The ones with light eyes or "good hair." If you fit the
mold of being conventionally attractive by colorism's
standards, then you were rewarded. All the boys
wanted to date you, and all the girls wanted to be your
friend. I can recall wanting to be friends with the
pretty light skin girls in my class in elementary
school. My proximity to them made me feel
validated. Something about having a personal
relationship with a conventionally attractive person
makes us feel like we can absorb some of their pretty
privileges. In the same way that many people of color
feel like their personal relationships with white
people lessen the blow of racism. Both are false.

I spent a good chunk of my childhood thinking that if
I were white or biracial, people would think I was
beautiful too. I didn't want to be sexually appealing; I
wanted to be admired like my light/white peers and
the girls I saw on TV. I learned quickly that sexual
attraction is fluid, and it doesn't take much for a male

to show interest in you sexually. So that never mattered to me. However, there was a significant difference in how boys treated the girls they genuinely found attractive. Those girls were treated with respect and kindness. Not just by our peers but even by the adults around us. It's one thing when you notice the boys at school treating you differently, but it's another when you see it from your superiors. Being called ugly by an adult—a family member and a teacher especially, rips you up inside and leaves a mark of emotional damage that never truly goes away.

So much so, that any efforts you make to improve your appearance never take the insecurities away. No amount of relaxers, weaves, makeup, and cute outfits made up for the fact that I never felt like I was enough. So eventually, I gave up. I gave up my efforts of seeking validation from others. I gave up trying to be the prettiest girl in the room and eventually lived as if the room no longer existed. I won't pretend that this was easy. Or that I still don't struggle with moments of seeking validation from others. My body dysmorphia is something that developed as a child, due to the cold, prejudice, and unsympathetic environment I had to grow up in. It will never entirely go away. There are times when it lies dormant, but it's never gone.

And some might even consider me privileged, considering I've had the same partner for almost 14 years. Navigating your insecurities as a black woman is one thing, but navigating them as a single woman is an entirely different experience. Whether people admit it or not, everyone wants to feel loved. It's easier to escape that "room" when you have someone by your side who thinks the entire world revolves around you. And while I'm thankful for that, I refuse to attach my confidence to someone else. With or without a romantic partner, at the end of the day we still have to face the fact that you exist as an individual in a world that hates you just for existing.

While writing this book, I scrolled Pinterest for some body-positive inspiration. Instead, I was bombarded by cheesy quotes plastered on repetitive images and illustrations of women with pink underarm hair, a little stomach flab, and stretch marks. *(With a small percentage of those graphics being dark/brown-skinned women of color.)* The same old shit you've seen and heard a million times. I've begun to question how effective this method of performative feminism has become. Who is it all really for? Is your allyship beneficial when fat women still face medical discrimination? When Black women still face threats and harassment just for existing in media? At what point do we stop fucking around with corny ass insta-graphics and start demanding real change? Get it together, girl. This shit ain't gonna dismantle itself.

**Don't forget to leave a review on Amazon,
Goodreads, or Hardy Publications Facebook page!**

About the Author

YA/NA author and poet born and raised in the
Washington D.C. area. In 2017 Chanel decided to
take a leap of faith and follow her dreams of
publishing her first book, *'My Colorblind Rainbow'*
which made the 'In The Margins Award Long List' for
YA fiction in 2018. She launched Hardy Publications
in September of 2017, working as a freelance writer
and literary blogger. She's written for publications
such as *Women and Words, 25 Hottest Indie Authors
Artists Advocates 2020, and CulEpi.* She is also the
editor-in-chief of *COFFEE WINE & WORDS
Literary Magazine.*
With certifications in persuasive writing and public
speaking, TEFL(Teaching English as a Foreign
Language) while overseas, Chanel uses her platform
to raise awareness for different charities and non-
profit organizations, volunteering both locally and
internationally, and giving back to the community.

IG and Twitter: @chanelhardypub_
Facebook: Hardy Publications
Also check out coffeewinewordsmag.com

Check out COFFEE WINE & WORDS Poetry Podcast on Spotify and other platforms!

Check out other poetry books by Chanel!

Sweet Oleander: A Collection of Poetry

Delicate: A Collection of Poems

I Had a Dream About You: A Collection of
Poems

www.ingramcontent.com/pod-product-compliance
Lightning Source LLC
Chambersburg PA
CBHW031632040426
42452CB00007B/795